FORGOTTEN YOUTH

Incarcerated Youth

Stephanie Watson

ReferencePoint
Press®

San Diego, CA

About the Author

Stephanie Watson is a freelance writer based in Providence, Rhode Island. For nearly two decades, she has covered the latest health and science research for WebMD, Healthline, and Harvard Medical School. Watson has also authored more than two dozen books for young adults, including *The Escape from Alcatraz* and *Brain Injuries in Football*.

For more information, contact:
ReferencePoint Press, Inc.
PO Box 27779
San Diego, CA 92198
www.ReferencePointPress.com

LIBRARY OF CONGRESS CATALOGING-IN-PUBLICATION DATA

Names: Watson, Stephanie, 1969- author.
Title: Incarcerated youth / by Stephanie Watson.
Description: San Diego, CA : ReferencePoint Press, Inc., 2017. | Series:
   Forgotten youth | Includes bibliographical references and index.
Identifiers: LCCN 2016021503 (print) | LCCN 2016027385 (ebook) | ISBN
   9781601529824 (hardback) | ISBN 9781601529831 (eBook)
Subjects: LCSH: Juvenile detention--United States--Juvenile literature. |
   Juvenile corrections--United States--Juvenile literature. | Juvenile
   delinquents--Rehabilitation--United States--Juvenile literature.
Classification: LCC HV9104 .W4247 2017 (print) | LCC HV9104 (ebook) | DDC
   365/.608350973--dc23
LC record available at https://lccn.loc.gov/2016021503

Contents

Introduction

Locked Up and Alone

Ismael Nazario grew up in Brooklyn, New York. His mother raised him alone, but she instilled in him the importance of getting a good education. And for a while, Nazario did well in school. He dreamed of becoming an architect or archaeologist. Then, when he was thirteen, his mother was diagnosed with breast cancer. As she underwent treatment with chemotherapy and radiation, the former good student fell in with the wrong crowd. His grades began to slip. He started smoking pot.

At age sixteen Nazario was charged with assault after getting into a fight. In New York a sixteen-year-old can be charged as an adult and held in an adult prison. While awaiting trial, Nazario was sent to Rikers Island jail. Rikers Island sits on a 415-acre (168 ha) island in the middle of the East River, between the boroughs of Queens and the Bronx. It houses about twelve thousand adults and hundreds of teenagers. Rikers is notorious for incidents of violence and abuse—both by inmates and its guards. Young people are especially vulnerable. "For adolescent inmates, Rikers Island is broken," says Preet Bharara, US attorney for the Southern District of New York. "It is a place where brute force is the first impulse rather than the last resort, a place where verbal insults are repaid with physical injuries, where beatings are routine, while accountability is rare."[1] As Nazario rode, shackled, in the blue and white correction department bus over the bridge to Rikers Island, he thought, "What did I get myself into?"[2]

The area of Rikers that houses teens is nicknamed "Gladiator School." The kids are tough, and they do everything they can to prove it. Less than three days after Nazario's arrival, four inmates jumped him. They wanted his phone privileges and his snacks from the commissary—the prison store. They ordered him to ask their permission every time he wanted to use the bathroom.

Solitary Confinement

To punish young inmates who misbehave, or to protect them from violence and sexual assault from adult inmates, prisons often place teens in solitary confinement. Nazario was thrown into solitary for fighting and having tobacco. Out of the four hundred days he was at Rikers Island, he spent three hundred of them in solitary confinement. The cell where he was held is known as the box. It measured just 6 feet by 8 feet (1.8 m by 2.4 m)—about the same size as the interior of a minivan. Inside its cinder block walls were a bunk, sink, and toilet. Guards delivered food through a slot in the metal door. Mice and roaches often skittered across the floor. In the summertime, the cell would get so hot that the walls and floor appeared to sweat.

Nazario was confined to this tiny room for twenty-three hours a day. He was allowed out only for showers and for brief recreational periods outdoors while inside a chain-link cage. With little to do inside his small cell, Nazario often paced back and forth, talking to himself. Sometimes he hallucinated. He feared he would lose his mind. The sounds inside his head would be drowned out by the screams of other boys coming from neighboring cells. "You just get angry with hearing people constantly hollering all day,"[3] he says. To hold on to whatever sanity he had left, Nazario read. He also wrote music and short stories.

> "For adolescent inmates, Rikers Island is broken."[1]
>
> —Preet Bharara, US attorney for the Southern District of New York.

Lost in the System

Nazario was one of the estimated fifty-four thousand young people who are held within the US criminal justice system on any given day. Most of these youths are placed in juvenile detention facilities, correctional facilities, or group homes. About six thousand are housed in adult jails.

Inmates file out of the Rikers Island jail bakery after working the morning shift. Teen inmates, who are far outnumbered by adults at the New York City jail, are especially vulnerable to violence and abuse.

Although the public perceives incarcerated youth to be kids too dangerous to be left on the streets, most young people who end up in jail have not committed violent crimes. Two-thirds are there for drugs, theft, probation violations, or status offenses like running away or breaking curfew.

Most young people who end up in prison started out disadvantaged. They spent their early lives in poverty-stricken homes in violence-ridden neighborhoods. Many were raised in broken homes by a single parent or another relative. Or their real families could not care for them, and they were shuttled from one foster family to another. A large percentage of incarcerated youths suffer from substance abuse, mental health issues, and/or learning disabilities that have not been properly treated. Many were physically or sexually abused at home or while in foster care.

Once young people enter the prison system, they are not only locked away but also forgotten by the world around them. They have limited access to friends and family, who often do not have the transportation to visit them in jail or the money to pay for collect phone calls from prison. Young inmates who let their guard down enough to make new friends in a correctional facility run the risk of becoming victims of gang violence or sexual abuse.

Unable to Break Free

While incarcerated, young people may not have access to the same quality education as their peers in public schools. Many facilities, especially adult prisons, offer limited or no help for kids with learning disabilities, mental health issues, or substance abuse problems.

Once kids are released from prison, they can get lost in a system that is poorly equipped to handle them. Many are sent back into the same troubled homes and dangerous communities that drove them into prison in the first place. Even kids who want to succeed after their release find it difficult because their criminal record makes it almost impossible for them to get into college, rent an apartment, or find a job. With no educational and career options available to them and a lack of adult supervision to steer them in the right direction, many kids see no option other than to go back to the life they used to lead. "While I was in prison, I used to hear dudes talking about when they get released from prison, what type of crimes they're gonna commit when they get back in the street," Nazario says. "I called it a go-back-to-jail-quick scheme."[4]

Today the government and nonprofit organizations are working to change the future for incarcerated youth. They offer services to

"What did I get myself into?"[2]

—Ismael Nazario, a former teen inmate at Rikers Island.

help kids transition from prison back into the world, find safe and affordable housing, and avoid reincarceration. Now in his twenties, Nazario has devoted his life to helping other kids succeed after prison. He works as a case manager for the Fortune Society, which connects troubled teens with the services they need to re-enter society after incarceration. He hopes for a future in which teens will make better choices, and those who do make mistakes will not face such harsh punishment. "If I was to see my 15-year-old self today, I would sit down and talk to him and try to educate him," Nazario says. "Keep your behind in school, man, 'cause that's where you need to be 'cause that's what's going to get you somewhere in life. This is the message we should be sharing with our young men and women. We shouldn't be treating them as adults and putting them in cultures of violence that are nearly impossible for them to escape."[5]

Chapter 1

The Path from School to Prison

Although the rate of youth imprisonment has dropped by about half since the mid-1990s, the United States still locks up more teenagers than any other developed nation. On any given day about fifty-four thousand youths are held within the criminal justice system.

The way the US government processes and treats juvenile offenders has changed dramatically over the years. During the eighteenth century the colonial justice system viewed children as mini adults. A child as young as seven years old could stand trial—and be convicted—in an adult court. Children who were convicted of murder could even be sentenced to death.

When it came to trying and sentencing children, the American courts drew much of their influence from England's courts, and especially from a highly respected British lawyer named William Blackstone. Blackstone wrote that "the capacity of doing ill, or contracting guilt, is not so much measured by years and days, as by the strength of the delinquent's understanding and judgment."[6] Blackstone went on to say that a child under seven cannot be found guilty of a crime because he is not able to understand what he has done wrong. But at eight years old, a child is aware enough to be found guilty.

Three centuries ago children were sometimes put in prison simply because there was no other place for them. So many children were poverty-stricken and neglected that towns did not have anywhere to house them other than in adult prisons. There, they were locked up in overcrowded cells, surrounded by violent and mentally ill adults.

According to the most recent figures available, an estimated fifty-four thousand young people are being held within the US criminal justice system. Most of these youths are housed in juvenile prisons. About six thousand are held in adult prisons. Many of the incarcerated youths are being held temporarily until their court hearing or placement. Accurate counts of youths housed within state justice systems are hard to find, because states do not always report every youth offense. The information presented here is based on the state in which the youths committed their offenses.

WA 1,014
OR 1,086
MT 150
ID 450
ND 171
MN 939
WI 816
MI 1,683
NH 78
VT 27
ME 162
NY 1,650
MA 393
RI 159
CT 279
NJ 888
SD 333
WY 165
IA 735
IL 1,617
IN 1,581
OH 2,283
PA 2,781
DE 159
DC 228
MD 771
NV 591
UT 612
CO 1,077
NE 411
KS 885
MO 1,053
KY 774
WV 510
VA 1,563
NC 543
CA 8,094
AZ 882
NM 402
OK 519
AR 681
TN 666
SC 672
MS 243
AL 933
GA 1,557
TX 4,383
LA 774
FL 2,802
AK 195
HI 78

Source: Office of Juvenile Justice and Delinquency Prevention, "Placement Status by State, 2013." www.ojjdp.gov.

The Push for Rehabilitation

By the late 1800s a group of reforming psychologists and sociologists began to argue that prison was not the right place for children. Kids were not miniature adults, they said. Instead of imprisoning troubled youth, the government needed to rehabilitate them. A group of wealthy philanthropists and prison reformers, including Thomas Eddy and John Griscom, founded the Society for the Reformation of Juvenile Delinquents. The organization charged itself with looking out for the good of America's poor and wayward youth—and moving children out of adult prisons. The society led to the creation of the country's first juvenile reformatory—the New York House of Refuge—to house and rehabilitate poor, troubled young people before they could turn into juvenile delinquents. In this reformatory, children had to follow a strict daily schedule and faced harsh discipline if they misbehaved. Yet it was not as over-crowded, abusive, or dangerous to children as the nation's adult prison system.

In 1899 Illinois passed the Juvenile Court Act, which created the country's first juvenile court to process young offenders. The goal was to separate youths, who were still young enough to be rehabilitated, from hardened adult criminals. By 1925 juvenile courts operated in almost every state. In the 1950s and 1960s, the juvenile court process underwent some changes. It became more formal—operating much like adult trials. Witnesses were introduced, and youths were given the right to be represented by an attorney. Young people who had committed minor offenses were given different penalties than those who committed serious offenses. The Juvenile Justice and Delinquency Prevention Act of 1974 provided states with funds to develop community-based programs to keep kids who had committed minor offenses out of jail. The act also required jailed juveniles to be kept separate from adult prisoners for their own protection.

A gentler approach to youth offenders, with its emphasis on rehabilitation rather than incarceration, continued through much of the mid-twentieth century. Then, in the 1980s and 1990s, the tide turned as Americans began to see an increasing number of television reports spotlighting youth violence. The teens who were perpetrating the murders and other violent acts reported on the news were labeled as superpredators. Criminologists called these teens "brutally remorseless" and "radically impulsive."[7] They warned of a "bloodbath of teenage violence."[8] The public became worried that the justice system was going too easy on youths who committed violent crimes. In an effort to protect the public, lawmakers cracked down on young offenders. The gov-ernment made it easier for children to be tried in adult courts and to receive harsher sentences. Some states allowed children as young as sixteen or seventeen to be tried and convicted as adults.

The Prison Pipeline

Although the public perception may be that most young offenders are violent and dangerous, less than one-quarter of youths in jail have committed a violent crime, and just 1 percent were arrested for murder. The majority of young people are locked up for non-violent offenses, such as drug or alcohol possession, probation violation, truancy (skipping school), or theft.

Often kids land in prison due to a mistake that resulted from a difficult circumstance. "The majority of kids [in juvenile jail] are victims," says Richard Ross, a professor at the University of California, Santa Barbara, who interviewed more than one thousand youths in over three hundred detention centers. "They don't wake up one day and decide they're going to be criminals. A kid might be smoking weed on a Friday night and all of a sudden their life spirals down."[9]

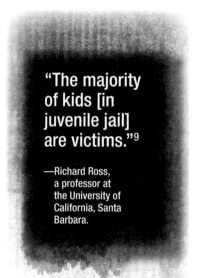

"The majority of kids [in juvenile jail] are victims."[9]

—Richard Ross, a professor at the University of California, Santa Barbara.

Many of the kids who end up in prison started out in impoverished or volatile families. A third of them grew up in low-income public housing. In 2014 the poverty rate for children under age eighteen was 21 percent, according to the US Census Bureau. Kids who grow up in poverty are more likely to commit a crime than those from wealthier families. Many poor children are raised in single-parent households, where they might not get the care and attention they need to stay out of trouble. Research finds that children from single-parent homes are more likely to be arrested than those who grow up in two-parent homes.

Adolfo Davis came from a broken family in Chicago. His mother was addicted to crack. His father was out of the picture. Davis's care was left to his grandmother, who worked full-time and was

Most young offenders do not end up in jail because of violent crimes. The majority of incarcerated youth are there because of nonviolent crimes such as drug or alcohol possession, probation violations, truancy, or theft.

already taking care of a sick husband and a mentally disabled son. With little to eat in the house, Davis started stealing food to quiet his rumbling belly. At age ten, after taking a few dollars' worth of food stamps, he was sent to Audy Home—a juvenile detention center. After his release, he fell in with the Gangster Disciples, a gang from Chicago's South Side. "I loved them, they protected me, they were my family,"[10] he says. Two years later, in 1990, he was with two older gang members when they broke into a rival gang's house and shot and killed two people. Even though he had not pulled the trigger, Davis was sentenced to life in prison without parole. He was just fourteen years old. Over the last twenty-five years, Davis has fought to overturn his sentence, but so far he remains in jail.

Violence and abuse often go hand in hand with poverty. Six out of ten first-time offenders are in the child welfare system because they were abused or maltreated at home. Nearly 50 percent of boys and more than 76 percent of girls who are sentenced to life in prison were physically abused. Mayra, a seventeen-year-old

The New York House of Refuge

In the early 1800s, children who were charged with a crime, no matter how minor, were sentenced to adult prisons. In these overcrowded institutions, young people lived side by side with hardened criminals and the mentally ill.

A group of wealthy businessmen and prison reformers, including a Quaker named John Griscom, believed adult prisons were no place for children. They established the New York House of Refuge—the country's first juvenile reformatory. In 1825 it opened in New York City with six boys and three girls. Most of the children were there for minor offenses like running away from home. By 1854 the House of Refuge had expanded to eight hundred youths, ages eight to seventeen. To accommodate its growing population, the facility moved to a larger space on Randall's Island in the East River.

For children who lived in the House of Refuge, days were long and regimented. They were awakened at sunrise. After morning prayers and classes, they worked from 7 a.m. until 5 p.m., with breaks only for breakfast and lunch. Boys made shoes, chair frames and seats, and caps. Girls did the washing, cooking, and housework. Then it was back to school until 8 p.m.

The House of Refuge served as a model for other youth reformatories around the country. But over time new state institutions opened, including the New York Reformatory for Women and the State Training School for Boys. As youths transferred to these institutions, the House of Refuge's population dwindled. By 1935 the country's first youth reformatory had shut its doors forever.

who is serving a life sentence in California, says her father used to hit her with horsewhips until her back bled. "After he used to hit me or whip me, he would tell me, 'Don't cry, why you crying, I'm gonna hit you harder.'. . . So I had to hold my tears in and it built up."[11]

A history of sexual abuse is also common among kids who end up in prison. "I'd been molested for years," says eighteen-year-old Elizabeth, who was awaiting sentencing for running away from home. "Finally I told my grandmother about it. That it was my stepfather. She called the cops and I ran away and right before he was supposed to go to court he shot himself in the head."[12]

Difficulties in School

Many imprisoned kids had difficulty in school. About a third of incarcerated teens have a learning or emotional disability. Schools are supposed to address these kids' special needs, but they do not always do so. "Kids with learning disabilities that are not properly remediated in a school setting start to dislike school, or act up at school, or do things to distract from the fact that they're not doing well,"[13] explains Diane Smith Howard, senior staff attorney for the National Disability Rights Network.

School policies have also contributed to the problem of youth incarceration. Since the 1990s schools have ratcheted up punishments, instituting zero-tolerance policies that require mandatory suspension or expulsion for offenses like fighting or bringing a weapon such as a pocketknife to school. Cody Beck, who has bipolar disorder, lost his temper during an argument with a fellow student at Grenada Middle School in Mississippi and hit a few teachers who attempted to break up the argument. Beck was arrested and handcuffed in front of his classmates. He was charged with assault and was not allowed to return to school. Once children like Beck are suspended or expelled from school, they are more likely to be arrested, a phenomenon some experts call the school-to-prison pipeline. Minority students face a higher risk of entering this pipeline than white students, in part because research finds they are punished more harshly than white students. Black students are three and a half times more likely to be suspended from school than white students, which increases their likelihood of ending up in prison.

Most of the young people who wind up in prison are male minorities. Teenage boys are about sixteen times more likely to be incarcerated than girls. African American teens are nearly five times more likely than white teens to go to prison, and they are nine times more likely to be sentenced to an adult prison. The rate of imprisonment is also higher among Hispanic youths than among whites.

Where Do Incarcerated Youth Live?

The criminal justice system has a method for processing young offenders. When young people are arrested, the juvenile court's intake department reviews their cases. The intake department can decide to dismiss a case, or it can refer the child to a social service or mental health agency for help. If the behavior or crime is serious enough, and if the youth is likely to commit another crime or skip the court date, the intake department will usually recommend that he or she be placed in a locked detention or residential facility while awaiting trial.

Every day more than twenty thousand young people await trial in a detention center. Although they might spend only a couple of weeks at one of these facilities, that brief stay has long-lasting implications. Youth in detention centers are more likely to be formally charged with a crime and sentenced to jail than those who stay at home while awaiting their sentencing, in part because they don't receive the rehabilitation services they need to help them stay out of trouble.

After their trials, youths who are sentenced can be housed in either a secure or nonsecure facility. Secure facilities are essentially jails—buildings surrounded by tall, razor wire–topped fences, with locked cells that prevent inmates from escaping. Most young people charged with a crime are placed in juvenile facilities. About six thousand of them are incarcerated in adult prisons. Often these correctional facilities are located far away from the children's homes.

Nonsecure facilities have no fences or locks. They are often located within communities. Although kids have to follow a set of rules, the goal is to rehabilitate and reintegrate them back into society using educational programs, mental health and substance abuse therapies, and other social services. An example of a nonsecure program is day treatment—a facility where offenders must report five or more days a week for rehabilitation services, but they can return home at night. A smaller number of kids who have committed minor offenses are put under house arrest, in which they stay in their homes but have to follow certain rules. Or they may be placed in a group or foster home if their own family can-

Inmates at a youth correctional facility in Michigan must pass through many locking doors on their way to the cafeteria at mealtime. Most young people charged with crimes are sent to juvenile facilities, some of which closely resemble adult prisons.

not properly care for them. Another option is a youth detention camp, which is run more like a military boot camp than a summer camp. For between three and six months, the young people sentenced to these camps follow a rigorous schedule of disciplinary training, physical conditioning, work, and educational programs.

Serving Time—and Time Again

How long kids stay locked up depends on the severity of their offense. For minor crimes, they may have to do just a few hours of community service. Those who commit the most serious crimes, even at a young age, face the prospect of decades—or even an entire lifetime—in prison. The United States is the only country in the world that sentences children under eighteen to life in prison without parole.

Young people who get a life sentence can spend their entire lives paying for the mistakes they made as adolescents. Colt Lundy was fifteen years old when he was charged with the murder of his stepfather, Philip Danner. In 2010 he was sentenced to twenty-five years in the Wabash County Correctional Facility in Indiana. "I never thought I could actually go to prison," Lundy says. "I just thought the worst would be probation or boys' school, but you don't realize until after the fact that every decision you make, every choice has a repercussion, whether good or bad."[14]

> "You don't realize until after the fact that every decision you make, every choice has a repercussion."[14]
>
> —Colt Lundy, sentenced to twenty-five years in prison at age fifteen.

Prison does not always end once a sentence has been served. In many cases young people who are released from jail commit another crime and get arrested again. This tendency to reoffend is called recidivism. Certain factors make kids more likely to commit new crimes and end up in jail again. Youths who are held in adult prisons or who are in the child welfare system because of troubles at home are more likely to go back to prison. Those who do not have access to counseling, education, and programs to improve their life and work skills are also more likely to go back to jail. "In my eyes, my son went from a sixteen-year-old child to a thirty-year-old man overnight, absent the completed brain development. In his own eyes, he had no other choice but to go from a child to a man overnight to cope with his new surroundings," comments Keela Hailes, the mother of a youth offender. "He served out his sentence, came home and

A Life Cut Short

Kalief Browder was arrested in the spring of 2010 for stealing a backpack, which he insisted he had not taken. At sixteen years old, he was sent to Rikers Island, where he spent nearly three years awaiting trial because his parents could not afford the $10,000 bail money. For nearly two of those years he was in solitary confinement. During his stay at Rikers, Browder was repeatedly beaten, both by officers and by his fellow inmates. One surveillance video captured a group of prisoners hitting and kicking him over and over again.

Browder's desperation grew so extreme that he tried to kill himself more than once. In 2012 he tore up a bed sheet and used the pieces to fashion a noose. He tried to hang himself from the light fixture in his cell but did not succeed.

In 2013 Browder's case was dismissed without a trial, and he was released from prison. He started taking classes at Bronx Community College and seemed to be getting his life back on track. Yet he still suffered from depression, anger, and paranoia and was taking antipsychotic drugs to control his mood. "I'm mentally scarred right now. That's how I feel. Because there are certain things that changed about me and they might not go back," he said. On the evening of June 5, 2015, Browder told his mother, "Ma, I can't take it anymore." The next day, he committed suicide at his parents' home in the Bronx. Browder was twenty-two years old.

Quoted in Eyder Peralta, "Kalief Browder, Jailed for Years Without Trial, Kills Himself," NPR, June 8, 2015. www.npr.org.

Quoted in Jennifer Gonnerman, "Kalief Browder, 1993–2015," *New Yorker*, June 7, 2015. www.newyorker .com.

tried to be a productive member of society; however, two years later, he reoffended and was sent back to jail."[15]

Because states keep their own records of youth recidivism, experts do not know exactly how many juveniles end up back in jail nationwide. Yet state studies show that about 55 percent of youths are rearrested within one year of leaving prison. About 24 percent are imprisoned again.

Prison Consequences

The consequences of serving time continue long after young people are released from prison. Incarceration has a lifetime impact on a person's education, mental health, and employment opportunities. Young people who have been incarcerated are less likely than their peers to finish high school and attend college. Having a criminal record makes it harder for them to get a stable job, which is why teens who have been incarcerated ultimately earn less money during their careers than kids who have not been in prison.

According to the National Research Council of the National Academies, incarcerating young people interferes with their normal brain development and mental health. Teens who have been imprisoned are more likely than their peers to be depressed. The pressures and restrictions of prison drive young inmates to commit suicide at a rate two to three times higher than that of young people in the general population.

Most kids who go to prison end up there because of troubles at home, including poverty, abuse, and neglect. In prison, young people lose the freedoms they once took for granted. And once they have entered the juvenile criminal justice system, they can find it hard to leave it and get back on a path to a more promising future.

"In my eyes, my son went from a sixteen-year-old child to a thirty-year-old man overnight, absent the completed brain development."[15]

—Keela Hailes, mother of a youth offender.

Chapter 2

Freedom Lost

In prison, teens are no longer free to play sports, text with their friends, wear the types of clothes they like, or even sleep and eat when they want. Their lives become strictly ordered and regimented the moment they arrive and go through the receiving process. First, they are bused to the prison or detention center while shackled in handcuffs. A police officer stays with them throughout the journey. Once they arrive, teens have to remove all jewelry, shoes, belts, and any personal items in their pockets. They may also be strip-searched to make sure they have not brought in any weapons or other contraband. At this moment, all hopes of privacy and modesty disappear. "You get totally naked in front of whoever is there. You face the guard that is strip searching you and you hold your hands and arms up so they can see that you don't have anything in your hands or taped to your armpits," recalls an inmate in a Florida prison. After the guards searched his mouth and hair, he says, it was time to turn around:

> You pick up your feet one at a time to show that you don't have anything taped to the bottom of your feet. Lastly, you bend over and cough. The guard inspects your butthole to see if he thinks you have any drugs or weapons stuffed in there. If they think you have something in there, they do a cavity search on you immediately so you don't have a chance to get rid of it.[16]

New prisoners also have to shower before entering prison. That experience can be even more uncomfortable for young people placed in an adult prison. At age seventeen, Jabriera Handy was held in the Baltimore County Detention Center on charges of murder and assault after an argument led to her grandmother's death. "My first encounter with something bad would be me having to shower with a woman that was twice my age. My second encounter would be me having to squat and cough while on my menstrual,"[17] she recalls.

A new arrival submits to a search on entering a New Mexico detention center. The loss of personal freedom is made clear right at the start when young inmates are subjected to a search and ordered to relinquish all personal items.

After taking a shower, each new prisoner is issued underwear, socks, and a uniform, which may consist of either a striped or orange jumpsuit or a T-shirt and solid-colored pants. The prisoner is also given shoes. Laces are banned because they could be used to make a weapon or a noose to commit suicide.

Once young inmates have been thoroughly checked and processed, they are placed in a cell or a pod. In a juvenile facility, a pod is a dormitory-style area that contains several cells. Each cinder block–walled room is either a single or is shared by two or more roommates. The rooms are sparsely furnished with bunk beds, tables, and chairs, all of which are bolted to the floor or wall to prevent kids from throwing them. There may also be a small locker in which they can keep their personal items. The only splashes of color come from pictures the kids hang on the walls.

A small window in the room offers a glimpse at the world outside, but there is not much of a view. "I see the razor wire, the brick buildings. I'm thinking, 'Wow this is really prison.' It just really hits you,"[18] says Colt Lundy of his room at the Wabash County Correctional Facility in Indiana. Outside his window, guards and sharpshooters in towers keep a close watch, always alert for possible escapees.

> "I see the razor wire, the brick buildings. I'm thinking, 'Wow this is really prison.' It just really hits you."[18]
>
> —Colt Lundy, an inmate at Wabash County Correctional Facility in Indiana.

No Privacy

In prison, privacy is almost nonexistent. As inmates walk from their cells to places like the cafeteria or classrooms, guards monitor every move they make. At the Mohave County Juvenile Detention Facility in Arizona, "All activities and movements are supervised by Juvenile Detention staff including use of restrooms and showers and during sleeping periods,"[19] according to the facility's website.

Young people who share cells also share a toilet, which often sits in the middle of the room with no door or curtain around it. At Wabash, Lundy and his cellmates put up a sheet around the toilet whenever they want some privacy. There is also a communal bathroom with shower stalls and toilets, which looks like a public restroom. Swinging doors provide the only form of privacy while inmates shower or use the toilet. Some correctional facilities have cameras in the bathrooms, which are monitored by guards or administrators of the same gender as the inmates.

Beyond the embarrassment of having their bodies—and bodily functions—seen by other inmates or guards is the lack of personal space and time. "I'm so tired of being incarcerated. There's never a moment when I can have some privacy," one teen in jail complained in a blog post. "There are always other people around me. I just wish I could have 10 minutes alone in silence, but that's impossible in prison."[20] The only prisoners who do have complete privacy are those in solitary confinement.

Alone in a Cell

About six thousand young people are housed in adult prisons. To protect inmates under age eighteen against physical and sexual assaults by adult prisoners, facilities in many states keep them separated. Because of space constraints, often the way youths are separated is by placing them in solitary confinement. Both juvenile detention centers and adult jails also use solitary as a way to punish bad behavior.

Youths in solitary can spend twenty-two hours or more each day alone inside a cell with a solid steel door. Some solitary cells are so small that a teen who stretches out his arms can almost touch both walls at the same time. The only pieces of furniture are a narrow bed, a sink, and a toilet. Although there is no television, prisoners may get access to books and other reading materials. Some cells have a small window to let in light. The only human contact inmates have for much of the day is with the guard who checks in on them and brings them food or with inmates in neighboring cells, who yell to each other through the walls. The only time young people in solitary confinement are let out of their

Daily Prison Schedule

Life in a youth prison follows a very strict routine. Days are long and sharply defined. Here is an example of a day at the Henley-Young Juvenile Justice Center in Jackson, Mississippi:

5:00 a.m.	Wake-up call; kids clean their rooms
5:20 a.m.	Exercise program
5:40 a.m.	Shower and dress
7:30 a.m.	Breakfast
8:15 a.m.	Morning school classes begin
11:30 a.m.	Lunch break
1:30 p.m.	Afternoon classes
3:13 p.m.	Return to pod
4:15 p.m.	Dinner

Sunday, Tuesday, and Thursday:
6–7:30 p.m.   Noncontact visitation

Monday, Wednesday, and Friday:
Youth can make supervised three-minute phone calls

cells is to shower and to exercise for an hour a couple of times a week in the gym or yard. Young inmates can remain in solitary for weeks or even months.

During their time in solitary, young people cannot go to school. And often adult jails are not designed to provide any sort of education. "The physical set-up is such that they can't do schooling," explains Michele Deitch, an attorney and researcher from the University of Texas who has studied the conditions of incarcerated youth in Texas's adult prisons. According to Deitch, the young people at the Dallas County Jail were housed down a long hallway that contained a row of single cells with metal doors, which were separated from the adult cells by only a sheet hanging from the ceiling. She said there was no classroom space, and if kids

in the prison were to be taught, "it would have to be basically a teacher standing at the cell door. I can't envision that being a productive experience."[21]

Inmates in solitary also cannot get the mental health care and other services they need. They may not be able to see visitors either. Some young inmates who have been in solitary confinement say the worst part was that they were not able to hug their parents. Their parents feel the loss too. "I can't hug him or give him a kiss on the cheek or buy him a pop or a snack or anything," complains Sandra Medina. Her son, Andrew, was locked up in solitary at the maximum-security Colorado State Penitentiary for a carjacking and murder committed when he was fifteen. "He's alive, but it feels like he's not."[22]

Robert Richardson, who was confined to Harford County Detention Center in Maryland at age sixteen for manslaughter and firearms charges, wrote about his ten-month experience in solitary. "From day to day, it's always the same. Isolation, 24 hours a day. The light stays on, the door stays closed, no human interaction. I felt like an animal. I was always in the same cage." Many of the men around him were mentally ill, and they would scream all night. "I couldn't sleep, with the screams and the banging. . . . And the smells . . . smells of urine and feces from the others. They wouldn't bathe. They would lie in bed and defecate on themselves or sling their waste."[23]

Young people who spend a long time in solitary confinement can feel like they are losing their mind. "I started to see pictures in the little bumps in the walls," recalls Carter, who was incarcerated at age fourteen. "I started talking to myself and answering myself. Talking gibberish. I even made my own language."[24] Kenny, age seventeen, spent more than eighty days in solitary confinement at a juvenile correctional facility in Circleville, Ohio, after he was arrested for receiving stolen property. "They locked me in that little room with nothing," he says. "I wasn't even thinking straight, banging my head on the door and everything else. I was acting like a crazy person. . . . I had some of the roughest nights in there that I've ever had in my life."[25]

For an adolescent, time spent in solitary can have long-term effects. According to a 2012 report on youth in solitary confinement by the American Civil Liberties Union,

> "From day to day, it's always the same. Isolation, 24 hours a day. The light stays on, the door stays closed, no human interaction. I felt like an animal."[23]
>
> —Robert Richardson, an inmate at Harford County Detention Center in Maryland, on his time in solitary confinement.

This bare social and physical existence makes many young people feel doomed and abandoned, or in some cases, suicidal, and can lead to serious physical and emotional consequences. Adolescents in solitary confinement describe cutting themselves with staples or razors, hallucinations, losing control of themselves, or losing touch with reality while isolated.[26]

A Strict Schedule

Life in prison is extremely regimented. Kids are told when to wake up, what clothes to wear, what and when to eat, when they can go outside or call their parents, and when to sleep. They follow a strict schedule from the moment they wake up each morning to the moment they go to sleep at night. "Six o'clock in the morning we get up," said Elizabeth, eighteen, who was awaiting sentencing in a Los Angeles, California, prison. "We have about 4 or 5 minutes to get ready. Breakfast is at 7 o'clock. That's usually disgusting. Then we go to school for a couple of hours, go to lunch, go to school again, come back, eat dinner, we get one hour of recreation, take our showers."[27]

Young people who are in community-based residential programs do not need to follow a schedule this strict, but they do have restrictions. They may be required to visit a center every day for school or rehabilitation programs. Kids in home-based detention sometimes have to wear a tracking bracelet so corrections officers can monitor their movements. Or they may be required to check in with an officer throughout the day or week. Young people in home detention typically can leave their house only for essential activities, such as school or a doctor's appointment.

"Adolescents in solitary confinement describe cutting themselves with staples or razors, hallucinations, losing control of themselves, or losing touch with reality while isolated."[26]

—American Civil Liberties Union

Mealtime

Three times a day, prison inmates line up and walk in a row to the cafeteria for meals. They are handed a plastic tray that holds a different type of food in each compartment—vegetable, meat, noodles or bread, salad, and maybe dessert. Prisons spend as little as $1.50 per meal, so it is not surprising that inmates complain about the taste and quantity. "'Meatballs' in fluorescent gray sauce were actually the best thing rolling out of the kitchen and cause for excitement,"[28] writes Stephen Katz about the food during his stay at Michigan's Oakland County Jail.

A typical daily menu in prison might look like this:

Breakfast—One cup of cereal with milk, half a cup of canned fruit, half a cup of fruit juice, and one biscuit with gravy.

Lunch—An eight-ounce cup of soup, a bologna sandwich, pasta salad, coleslaw, and a container of milk.

Dinner—Three ounces of meatloaf with gravy, one cup of egg noodles, half a cup of green peas, two slices of white bread, and one piece of fruit.

Although prisons aim to give young people the nutritional balance and number of calories they need to stay healthy (around twenty-eight hundred calories per day) and dietitians review each prison's menu twice a year, hunger is a common complaint. "Within a week I dropped 11 pounds [4.9 kg] and within two weeks my ribs popped through as I shed another 10 [4.5 kg],"[29] Katz says. To beef up their daily meals, inmates can buy junk food like candy, beef sticks, and corn chips at the prison store—but only if their families have given them money to spend.

Cut Off from the Outside

Behind the barbed wire and locked steel doors of a juvenile or adult prison, teens are cut off from everything and everyone they once knew—including their families. "The worst part of being locked up is that a lot of things you love get taken away from you, such as your freedom, rights, family, friends, goals and dreams that you're looking forward to pursuing,"[30] comments Jonathan, sixteen, an inmate in a California correctional facility.

Connections with friends and family sometimes suffer. During their incarceration, teens can feel as though the people who were once closest to them have left them behind. "It felt like the whole world was going on without me, and I was stuck," says Elizabeth. "I have a little sister born after I started running away and I don't even know her."[31]

Young people are often placed in facilities that are hours away from their homes—too far for their families to reach on a bus, subway, or other form of public transportation if they do not have access to a car. According to a 2010 survey, most young people in residential placement have families that live an hour or more away. More than one-quarter said their families would have to travel three or more hours to visit them. The farther away from home a prisoner is sent, the lower the likelihood that his or her family will visit. A 2015 report from the Prison Policy Initiative found that nearly 50 percent of inmates who were incarcerated less than 50 miles (80 km) from their homes had received a visit in the last month, but just 26 percent of those whose homes were between 101 and 500 miles (163 and 805 km) away had gotten a visit.

Youths are allowed to call home a few times a week. Those calls are timed, and they are collect calls, meaning that the family has to pay. The cost for collect calls from prison cannot exceed .25 cents per minute due to regulations from the Federal Communications Commission, but other fees can be added. For a family with a very limited income, spending even a few dollars for each call might be more than they can afford. Joyce Cook, a day care worker, was once hit with a bill of $1,300 for her son's collect calls from youth prison.

> "The worst part of being locked up is that a lot of things you love get taken away from you, such as your freedom, rights, family, friends, goals and dreams that you're looking forward to pursuing."[30]
>
> —Jonathan, sixteen, an inmate in a California correctional facility.

A teenage jail inmate in Arizona uses his phone time to call his girlfriend. Maintaining connections with friends and family can be challenging with limited time for phone calls and visits.

Visits from Family and Friends

Prisons also have specific days and times when family, close friends, and members of the religious clergy can visit—usually an hour or two during the week and on weekends. Anyone who wants to visit must be on an approved list, go through a criminal background check, and be searched when they arrive to make sure they have not carried in any items that are not allowed (such as food, tobacco, or weapons). Some inmates who are in jail for more serious and violent crimes are allowed only to have non-contact visits for the safety of their visitors. Their parents, siblings, and other visitors have to sit behind a screen or window. They talk to each other on a phone. The glass that separates them prevents kids from hugging, kissing, or touching their parents and siblings during the visit.

Special Challenges for Girls in Prison

At just twelve years old, Jessica was confined to the Bernalillo County Juvenile Detention and Youth Services Center in Albuquerque, New Mexico, on battery charges. Jessica is one of thousands of girls ages eleven to seventeen who are incarcerated each year. She is also among the estimated 90 percent of young women in prisons who have been the victims of physical, sexual, or emotional abuse. Often that abuse continues once they are incarcerated—either at the hands of guards or their peer inmates. In prison, young women are also subject to strip searches and solitary confinement. These collective abuses often go unseen by the public, making girls "one of the most vulnerable and unfortunately invisible populations in the country," according to Catherine Pierce, a senior adviser at the federal government's Office of Juvenile Justice and Delinquency Prevention.

Young women like Jessica who have ended up in the criminal justice system may not receive the types of health and mental health care they need because programs are mainly targeted to males, who make up the bulk of the prison population. And because girls often do not receive the care they need while in prison, they face more mental health problems and other negative consequences once they are released.

Quoted in Jenny Gold, "Women's Health in Juvenile Detention: How a System Designed for Boys Is Failing Girls," *Atlantic*, November 28, 2012. www.theatlantic.com.

The tightly restricted schedule and limited time to spend with family and friends creates a sense of isolation. "My family came out twice this year. You have special visits, half an hour," says Elizabeth. "For the past year, I've seen someone I know from the outside for one hour, that's it. It's pretty hard being out here all by yourself."[32]

A lack of contact with loved ones can have a devastating effect on a prisoner's frame of mind—and future prospects. Joseph Maldonado was placed in a youth prison in Northern California for car theft. He was kept in isolation for two months and eventually went on a hunger strike that killed him. "If I could have visited or we were talking more, he could have gotten some of that off his head," his sister Renee Nuñez asserts. "I'm sure that would have helped."[33] Research finds that inmates who get more visits are also less likely to commit crimes once they are released. "[Visitation] gives them a stake in something on the outside that's important,"[34] says Nancy La Vigne of the Urban Institute, a public policy research group in Washington, DC.

In prison, young people cannot enjoy any of the freedoms they had on the outside. Their day is tightly controlled, they lose their privacy, and some are locked up in a tiny cell for twenty-two or more hours a day. During their time in prison, they are largely cut off from the people they love most. A lack of time for socialization, coupled with a fear of assault, also prevents young people from forging meaningful friendships with their fellow inmates.

Chapter 3

Finding Allies

The teenage years are a time for kids to explore their world through new social connections and friendships. The types of relationships they form during this period help shape their personality and have a strong influence on their future development. Making friends at this age can be a challenge, even for kids on the outside. In prison, real friendships are even harder to find. For one thing, opportunities for social interaction are limited or unavailable.

Adult prisons often place young people in solitary confinement, where they are alone for much of the day. About the only interaction they do have is with the adult guards. Juvenile facilities allow inmates an hour or two a day for group activities like playing basketball in the yard, watching television or playing cards in the common area, or taking part in classes such as Bible study or arts and crafts.

Even when young people have time to socialize, their peers are not always good influences. In prison, young inmates are often housed with gang members and repeat criminal offenders. "You got me in a place where I'm surrounded by nothing but gangs, so the only way not to be a victim of one of those gangs is to join them,"[35] says Ethan, who was incarcerated at age nineteen. Kids who try to fit in by adopting the behaviors they see around them are more likely to get in trouble again and get time in solitary confinement or be reincarcerated, a phenomenon researchers call peer contagion.

A Fear of New Friends

Along with having little time to cultivate new friendships, youth in prison hold back from making allies because they are mistrustful of the other inmates. Many of them have heard horror stories about violence and sexual assaults in prison. They keep to themselves out of fear that if they let their guard down, they will get beaten up or raped. Or they stay alone to avoid getting caught up in gangs or illegal activities that could add time to their sentence. When incarcerated youth do open up enough to make friends, it is usually with a small number of people they knew from their old neighborhood or they met during the intake process.

Inmates at a Wisconsin jail take part in a meditation class. One of the few opportunities for socializing occurs during scheduled group activities such as basketball, classes in meditation or arts and crafts, and Bible study.

Eventually the isolation becomes too much for some kids, and the walls they have built around themselves come down—if only a little bit. "It's just hard, because, I mean, when I went in there I tried to keep to myself, but you just get so lonely that, oh my God, I just want someone to talk to," says a young inmate named Alex. "I had just one friend in there. . . . I talked to him every day. . . . It got me through my time faster."[36]

Pseudofamilies

With their real families far away, some young people create their own network of prison relatives. Older inmates sometimes act as father figures to male inmates. "In many ways, I was raised in the prison system. I first learned to shave in the county jail at 16, a 65-year-old crack dealer showed me how," comments one young man who was jailed as an adult at age sixteen. "I grew up in here, and I am fortunate that I was taken in by older guys who were positive people. It could have been worse for me, and for many children now entering our prisons, it is worse."[37]

> "In many ways, I was raised in the prison system. I first learned to shave in the county jail at 16, a 65-year-old crack dealer showed me how."[37]
>
> —A young man who was jailed as an adult at age sixteen.

In women's prisons, female inmates often take on the roles of many different family members—mother, sister, grandmother, and aunt. These prison pseudofamilies can have fifteen or more members. Having a family on the inside—even with people who are not blood relatives—gives inmates a sense of security, eases their loneliness, and offers young people the kind of hands-on care their real families may not have provided at home.

Caren Sue was "adopted" by prison parents Daphne and Demona when she was jailed at age eighteen. "When I first started calling Daphne 'Mom,' I would catch myself. I felt disrespectful to my real mom who died when I was [a child]. . . . Now I think she would appreciate me having another mother figure,"[38] she says. Pseudofamilies

Pen Pals

With family far away and friendships hard to find in prison, many young inmates turn to the outside world for companionship. In 2009 Pennsylvania art store manager Cindy Sanford struck up a correspondence with a young prisoner named Kenneth Crawford. At fifteen, Crawford had been sentenced to life without parole in a state correctional facility for a double homicide. Crawford sent Sanford paintings he had made in prison. Impressed with his work, she sent him a Christmas card—the only one he received that year. She learned that he had not had a visitor in years and that his parents had abused him when he was a child. Sanford and Crawford began to write back and forth to one another. In 2010 Crawford sent Sanford a Mother's Day card. "You are a mother figure to me," it read. "I never had a mother in my life. It is really nice to have someone who cares."

Several programs, including the Pen Pal Ministry and PrisonInmates.com, facilitate pen pal friendships between people on the outside and youth incarcerated in prisons around the country. Some pen pal programs, like Black and Pink, find pen pals for specific groups of inmates, such as those who are lesbian, gay, bisexual, transgender, and questioning.

Quoted in Gary Gately, "Up from the Depths: Juvenile Offenders Who Turned Their Lives Around," Juvenile Justice Information Exchange, April 29, 2014. http://jjie.org.

are usually temporary, though. They often do not stick together once their members are released from prison.

Prison Gangs

Gangs are another type of surrogate family unit inside the juvenile prison system. Prison gangs serve the same purposes as street gangs. They offer their members protection and a sense of power. Like their counterparts on the outside, they make money illegally by selling contraband items like cigarettes and drugs that they have smuggled into the prison.

A young female gang member boards a jail bus after being arrested during a Los Angeles gang sweep. Incarcerated youth often join gangs for protection—which is the same reason frequently given for why youths join gangs on the outside.

The boundaries between street and prison gangs can be porous. Many members of prison gangs belonged to street gangs before their arrests, and they may go back to that same gang when they are released. Gang leaders have been known to direct outside activities from behind prison walls.

Prison gangs often band together by race or ethnicity. The Neta gang started in Puerto Rico and mainly consists of Hispanics. The Black Guerrilla Family, which was founded in California's

San Quentin State Prison, is made up of African Americans. Some gangs, like the white supremacist Aryan Brotherhood, use their race to separate themselves from other inmates and promote hatred.

New inmates can be recruited into gangs shortly after they arrive in prison. A gang leader may entice new members with promises of protection and privilege or threaten them into joining using fear and intimidation. Once gang members are initiated, they show their solidarity through tattoos (obtained illicitly in prison) or by flashing special signals to one another. Neta members, for instance, greet one another by crossing the fingers of their right hand over their heart in a show of unity. "The way they stand, the way they hold their hands," explains Eric Gallon, the facility administrator at Cypress Creek Correctional Facility in Florida. "They communicate with their hands."[39]

Prison gangs earn credibility and respect through violence. Fights between rival gangs are common. Sometimes gang leaders order so-called hits on other prisoners or on prison guards as a show of their strength. The Heartless Felons, one of the largest gangs in Ohio, have become known for their ruthless attacks against other inmates and guards in both juvenile and adult prisons. In June 2013 at the Scioto Juvenile Correctional Facility in Delaware County, Ohio, members of the Heartless Felons jumped guards who were trying to break up a fight at a pickup basketball game. When one of the gang members was asked why he had attacked the guards, he said, "They were messing with my boys." He added, "They should have stayed out of it."[40] In 2012 gang members beat up a female corrections officer at the same facility. They gave the officer a concussion, broken nose, and eye injuries severe enough to land her in the hospital.

Prison Violence

Violence is an ever-present threat for youth in prison. It is considered a rite of passage for new inmates. That may be why one report found that 42 percent of young people in prison live in fear of being attacked. "In a sense, it became natural to walk down the hall and see somebody getting beat up," recalls Dwayne Betts, who served nearly nine years in a Virginia prison for a carjacking. "In a lot of ways, I think I was the exception in that I didn't get raped, I didn't get robbed."[41]

At Lancaster Correctional Institution, a youth prison in Florida, inmates call the ritual beatings a "test of heart." New arrivals are forced to endure painful assaults to gain the respect of their fellow inmates. Gesnerson Louisius, age nineteen, had just arrived in May 2013 when six inmates cornered him in an empty room. They held him down and hit him over and over again with primitive weapons fashioned from socks stuffed with bars of soap. Then they raped him with a broomstick. The attack, which lasted thirty minutes, left Louisius bloody and close to dead. "There isn't any doubt that they could have killed him. This wasn't a fistfight, and it wasn't the first attack that day, or that month. They were impaling people. It's like something out of the Middle Ages,"[42] says Louisius's attorney, Michael Sasso.

> "In a sense, it became natural to walk down the hall and see somebody getting beat up."[41]
>
> —Dwayne Betts, who served nearly nine years in a Virginia prison for carjacking.

Guards sometimes turn a blind eye to these assaults. Lee Arrendale State Prison in north Georgia used to be informally known as "gladiator school." John Lash, who was sent there at age eighteen after being sentenced to life in prison for murder, explains, "Though we didn't have organized combat, there was a culture among the prisoners and guards supporting the belief that violence was normal. Guards would often turn a blind eye to assaults, robberies, and other crimes. At times they would facilitate fights by letting inmates come together to settle their differences by combat."[43] (Today Arrendale is a women's prison.)

Rikers Island in New York is another prison notorious for its violence. When four inmates jumped Ismael Nazario during his stay there, an officer standing nearby was slow to break up the fight. After the fight ended, the guard asked Nazario if he was going to "hold it down,"[44] meaning that he would not report the incident.

Authorities display weapons confiscated from inmates at a California prison. Dangers abound even in youth prisons, where inmates often manage to fashion primitive weapons from commonly available items.

Guards at Rikers reportedly led a program that has been described as a fight club. To keep order, they offered special privileges—like commissary money—to inmates who were willing to beat up troublemakers. "It's how they keep control of things without having to get their hands dirty," a source told the *New York Post*. "I'd say there are about 15 to 18 fights a day there and more than 4,000 injuries each year."[45] In 2008 eighteen-year-old Christopher Robinson was beaten to death as part of this fight club while he was being held on a parole violation. At times, officers at Rikers have even perpetrated the violence against inmates. "[A] couple of individuals that [I] was close with I saw get [their] jaws broken by CO [correctional officer] captains . . . arms broken, ribs,"[46] Nazario recalled.

Sexual Assault

Young people in prison also live in fear of a different kind of abuse. Kids who enter correctional facilities become vulnerable to sexual

A Model Youth Facility

Youth prison programs are often places where young people are locked away and cut off from the world, a good education, and the social services they need to escape the prison system. Yet this is not so in the Nome Youth Facility, a program for young offenders in northwestern Alaska. Instead of spending their time in a solitary cell or following a strict regimen of school, work, meals, and sleep, kids who are housed at the Nome Youth Facility spend much of their time outdoors. They go on camping and fishing trips, ride bikes and dogsleds, and perform community service projects like planting flowers, working in the local food bank, or shoveling snow for older adults in the community.

At Nome, kids learn important life skills like cooking and carpentry, which they can use once they are released. Young people at the facility also have access to mental health therapy to help them deal with the abuse and other issues that caused them to get into trouble. Prison officials say caring for and nurturing these kids produces better outcomes—and behavior—than simply punishing them. "We treat them with dignity and respect," says superintendent Bob Froehle. "By doing so, we earn that in return."

Quoted in Alaska Department of Health and Social Services, Division of Juvenile Justice, "Nome Youth Facility." http://dhss.alaska.gov.

abuse—both by other inmates and the guards. In 2003 lawmakers passed the Prison Rape Elimination Act, which separates young people housed in adult prisons from the general population to protect them from sexual assault. Yet not all young people are kept separate, and assaults still happen. A seventeen-year-old inmate at the Richard A. Handlon Correctional Facility in Ionia, Michigan, was housed with an adult cellmate who raped him. The young inmate never reported the attack, "'cause he said he was going to stab me,"[47] he said. His cellmate had a weapon he had made from razor blades tied to a stick.

Sexual assaults against teens in juvenile prisons are even more common. In a survey of more than eighty-five hundred boys and girls in juvenile detention facilities, more than seventeen hundred said they had been sexually assaulted. Allen Beck, the Justice Department statistician who wrote the report, states that the rates of abuse by staff in juvenile prisons are "about three times higher than what we find in the adult arena."[48] Most kids have been victimized more than once, and the vast majority of them never report the abuse. "If they did they risked being further endangered, not just by their attackers, but by staff as well. Often when incidents were reported the authorities did little to stop it,"[49] comments Lash.

Because males make up the majority of the youth prison population, about 90 percent of the staff-on-inmate sexual abuse is perpetrated by women against young men, research finds. Female prison staff woo young prisoners with gifts and privileges—an extra portion of food, money for the commissary, or even drugs or alcohol. They also offer a caring ear whenever a prisoner misses his family or just needs to talk. It is a process known in the prison system as grooming.

One former inmate, who was incarcerated at a juvenile corrections center in Nampa, Idaho, when he was eighteen, recalled years later how the prison nurse flirted with him and gave him gifts of soda, candy, and money. Then she convinced him to have sex with her several times in the medical clinic. Being locked up made him more vulnerable to the nurse's assault. "You're an easy target," he says.[50] Sometimes the sex between female employees and young male inmates is forced using threats of punishment. Other times it is consensual. Either way, it is not accepted at youth prisons. And if the inmate is too young to give consent (that age varies from sixteen to eighteen by state), it is considered a form of rape.

The loneliness, distance from family and friends, and constant threats to their safety can weigh heavily on young people during their period of incarceration. Days spent locked inside prison walls can be long and empty. Friends and confidantes are hard to find among the hardened prison population. When inmates do let down their guard and trust their fellow inmates or prison staff, they become vulnerable to violence from prison gangs and sexual assault by staff—the very people who are charged with keeping them safe.

Chapter 4

Preparing for Life on the Outside

To have a chance at a promising future after prison, kids need an education. Young people who do not finish high school are less likely to find a job than their peers who graduate and go to college. According to a 2015 Bureau of Labor Statistics report, the unemployment rate among high school dropouts was 8 percent, whereas it was only 5.4 percent among high school graduates and 2.4 percent for college graduates. Even those dropouts who can get hired earn less money than people with more education. The average annual salary of a high school graduate is $35,000. Those who do not graduate earn an average of only $25,000.

Young people in prison have no chance of going to college if they cannot finish high school. Although juvenile facilities are required to offer high school programs, they often do not provide the same quality education as public schools. So when kids do leave prison, they may be way behind their peers academically. "Every day they're not getting a real education, then that's a day that we've lost," says Sue Burrell, a staff attorney at the San Francisco–based Youth Law Center. "The kids that are in juvenile justice can't afford to lose those days."[51]

Prison programs also graduate far fewer students than public schools. Only 9 percent of students in juvenile justice facilities were on track to earn a high school diploma or pass the equivalent General Educational Development (GED) test, according to a 2014 report from the Southern Education Foundation. And only 2 percent were accepted at and enrolled in college. These rates are much lower than graduation and college acceptance rates overall. In Louisiana about 8 percent of young people in prison earn high school credit compared to 36 percent of students in the state. "Way too many kids enter juvenile-justice systems, they don't do particularly well from an education standpoint while they're there, and way too few kids make successful transitions out,"[52] comments Kent McGuire, president and CEO of the Southern Education Foundation. A lack of money is not always to blame for this failure to graduate. Louisiana spends more than $16,000 a year to teach incarcerated students—more than three times the $5,300 it spends to teach its public school students.

Youths in adult prisons fare even worse. A Bureau of Justice Services survey found that 40 percent of adult jails provided no educational services to young inmates, and only 7 percent offered vocational, or job skills, training.

Education and vocational training in prison can lower the odds that young people will return to jail in the future. A 2013 study by the Rand Corporation found that prison education programs lower recidivism by about 40 percent and are cost-effective. For

A Florida juvenile detention center inmate takes a GED practice test. Studies show that education programs for incarcerated youth reduce recidivism.

every dollar that states spend on these programs, they save four or five dollars in reincarceration costs.

Given all the benefits, why are kids in prison not getting a better education? Learning issues, a lack of trained staff, and poor coordination during the transition from jail back to school may be partly to blame.

Learning Disabilities

Many youth offenders start out at an educational disadvantage. About 30 percent have learning disabilities that make it harder for them to read, pay attention, and learn as quickly as other students. Many of the young people in prison are at least two years behind their public school peers academically.

The Individuals with Disabilities Act of 2004 requires public schools to provide kids who have learning disabilities with an Individualized Education Plan (IEP)—a document that outlines their special learning needs and ensures that their school meets those needs. Even though youth prisons are also supposed to follow student IEPs, only about a third of young inmates get any kind of special educational services. "Kids with special needs are not being served well," complains David Domenici, director of the Center for Educational Excellence in Alternative Settings, which works to improve education in juvenile prisons. "My take is a lot of facilities don't thoughtfully look at the IEP."[53]

One nineteen-year-old who spent five months in a western Maryland youth prison camp says, "School was a joke." While in the program, he did not get the services that had been outlined in his IEP, including the extra help he needed with reading. "If the work is too hard for me, I'm not going to do it," he states. "Sometimes if I didn't do it, they would take me out of that class and put me in the dorm room [for] the rest of the class."[54]

Some kids leave prison without having made any academic progress. When Toney Jennings was arrested for statutory rape at age sixteen, he had a diagnosed learning disability and could barely read and write. Though he took high school classes at the Walnut Grove Youth Correctional Facility in Mississippi, he could not keep up because he did not have access to the special education he needed. By age twenty, Jennings was out of prison, but he was

A School Program That Works

Youth prisons have become known for the poor quality of education they provide incarcerated youth. But one Mississippi prison is considered a model for how prisons should teach kids. At Rankin County Juvenile Detention Center, teachers assess new students on the day they arrive. Lessons are then tailored to each student's ability level. About half of the kids in the prison school have an Individualized Education Plan to accommodate a learning disability.

Along with learning math, reading, and science, students take part in extracurricular activities like music therapy, art classes, or working in the center's greenhouse. At the end of each day, students get an hour of character education, where they learn positive moral, ethical, and behavioral skills. "That's the part of the day I look forward to the most is trying to mold these kids," teacher Daniel Wilburn says. "We're not going to save them all but if we can save a few, it's worth it." The prison's statistics tell the story of its success: between 2011 and 2013, its recidivism rate dropped nearly 8 percent.

Quoted in Sarah Butrymowicz, "Pipeline to Prison: How the Juvenile Justice System Fails Special Education Students," *Washington Monthly*, October 26, 2014. www.washingtonmonthly.com.

still illiterate and living with his grandmother. "If he hadn't gone to prison, I think he'd be reading by now," his grandmother Cornelia Glenn says. "He would have learned more. [Now] he'll always be dependent."[55]

A few youth prisons have tried to improve their educational programs. In 2003 three federal lawsuits were filed against the Oakley Youth Development Center in Raymond, Mississippi. In addition to charges that the center was treating inmates poorly, the lawsuits claimed that it had not provided required services—including education. The state's Division of Youth Services spent nine years working to improve conditions at the facility. Today most of the teachers there are certified in special education. A special education coordinator has also been hired to ensure that all kids with IEPs get the extra help they need.

A Lack of Teachers and Textbooks

One of the reasons why special education is not available to most youths in prison is because of a teacher shortage. Many teachers are afraid to work in what they see as a dangerous environment. "I've had a number of terrifying and heartbreaking days," writes Shannon, a teacher in a juvenile correctional center. "I've seen bloody brawls and received my fair share of insults."[56] Each morning before she can even get to her classroom, she has to go through a pat-down and then wait for prison staff to open seven locked doors for her.

> "I've had a number of terrifying and heartbreaking days. . . . I've seen bloody brawls and received my fair share of insults."[56]
>
> —Shannon, a teacher in a juvenile correctional center.

Teachers who are willing to assume the risks of working in a prison are often poorly trained to deal with special needs students. They also are not well supervised because there is no principal or other school administrator to oversee their work. In 2015 the National Association for the Advancement of Colored People filed a complaint against the Maryland State Department of Education program for juvenile offenders. The complaint claimed that young people in state custody were not getting a decent education, in part because many of their teachers were not properly certified.

Even when prison schools do hire qualified educators, those teachers may not have the tools they need to do their jobs. Textbooks in prison schools are often outdated and in short supply. Many prison classrooms lack basic school supplies like notebooks and pens. Some schools in juvenile facilities do not have the resources they need to follow the educational standards their state requires. As a result, the credits kids earn in jail may not count in public school once they are released.

Transitioning from Prison to High School

Once young people are released, a lack of coordination between the prison and high school can prevent them from transitioning

Students work on assignments in a language arts class at an Idaho juvenile detention center. Finding qualified teachers who are willing to work in a prison setting with youth who might have emotional and academic difficulties can be challenging.

back into the grade where they belong. The delivery of transcripts and records from prisons to schools can be slow and mired in bureaucratic red tape. Sometimes those records never make it to the school.

Without grades and other written evidence of the work students did while in prison, schools will not give them credit for completing the coursework. Because of missing records and concerns that prison educational programs are not up to state standards, high schools sometimes make kids repeat classes they already took. The poor-quality education in prison and lack of coordination between prisons and high schools may be one reason why two-thirds of kids do not return to school after their release.

Prison Vocational and Arts Programs

Because so many kids who are in prison will never finish high school or go to college, they need more than English, math, science, and history to get them on the road to a better life. Research finds that vocational training—learning real-world job skills—can help kids who do not plan to continue their education find employment and stay out of prison in the future.

Vocational programs in juvenile facilities teach young people many different types of job skills, including construction, cooking, graphic arts, computers, and electronics. While serving time for drug and weapons offenses at the Garden State Youth Correctional Facility in Yardville, New Jersey, Javier Herrera worked in the prison barbershop to earn credits toward his cosmetology license. He hoped that learning new skills like cutting and perming hair would help him get a job once he was eligible for parole. "Hair's always going to grow," he said. "It's something you can always make money off of."[57]

Some prisons also try to provide incarcerated youth with a creative education. Along with the core academic classes, they offer theater, art, and music programs. Studies find that prison art programs help foster creativity and self-expression, and they improve an inmate's motivation and life skills.

Young inmates at an Indiana juvenile detention center take part in a program aimed at teaching them to express themselves through art, music, and poetry. Programs like these improve motivation and life skills.

New Earth is a program in Los Angeles, California, that offers young men in juvenile probation camps classes in music, writing, poetry, art, and performance. New Earth says it costs just $3,500 a year to put a young person through its programs whereas it costs $125,000 annually to incarcerate a young person in the state. It also claims that its program has helped reduce recidivism rates among youths from 80 percent to less than 5 percent. "New Earth has changed my life in many ways," said Alex Pham, age twenty-one, a program graduate who found work as a camera operator for a company that showcases live animal cameras and documentary films. "It has changed the aspect of how I view the simplest things in life. The love, care, and appreciation the viewers have for the job I do is incredibly outstanding."[58]

Anger Management Programs

Other prison programs address the issues that landed young people in prison, including anger, substance abuse, and mental health problems. Studies find that managing these issues can help kids avoid ending up back in jail after they are released.

Trouble controlling anger is a common cause of assaults and other crimes. Some young people learned aggressive and violent behaviors at home or from their peers, and they never learned how to harness that anger. Once in prison, they express their rage and hopelessness through a bad attitude or by attacking other inmates or guards. "I couldn't deal with doing all that time, having that time, being so young, I couldn't deal with it," asserts a young man who was given a life sentence at age fifteen. "So there wasn't nothing I wouldn't do. Wasn't no fight I would back down from. Even with the officers. . . . [I was] stabbing officers with knives. . . . I've beat on inmates. . . . Yeah, I used locks, knives, pipes."[59]

Some youth correctional facilities offer anger management programs to help kids recognize negative emotions and learn healthier ways to express them. During these classes, young inmates develop problem-solving skills and gain the ability to see the world from other people's perspectives.

Substance Abuse Programs

About two-thirds of young people in prison have taken drugs, and many of them were arrested for that reason. Drug use can affect a person's judgment, making him or her more likely to commit crimes like assault, rape, or robbery. Many drugs are addictive, meaning that once someone starts taking them, he or she has a hard time stopping. Getting treated for drug abuse in prison reduces the odds that a young person will keep using and end up in prison again.

Prison drug treatment programs start by weaning the person off the substance to which he or she is addicted. Because this process often requires medicines, a doctor may be involved in the person's care. Young people also get counseling to combat the negative thoughts that drove them to use drugs. The goal is not only to get them off drugs but also to keep them off these substances permanently.

Mental Health Care

Up to 70 percent of young people in prison have at least one mental illness, yet just 20 percent of adolescents in the general population do. Many young inmates have been the victims of abuse and violence that left them emotionally scarred. Often mentally ill kids are locked up because the system does not know where else to put them. "We're seeing more and more mentally ill kids who couldn't find community programs that were intensive enough to treat them," explains Joseph Penn, the director of mental health services for the University of Texas Medical Branch Correctional Managed Care. "Jails and juvenile justice facilities are the new asylums."[60]

> "Jails and juvenile justice facilities are the new asylums."[60]
>
> —Joseph Penn, the director of mental health services for the University of Texas Medical Branch Correctional Managed Care.

Sixteen-year-old Donald was locked up in the Ohio River Valley Juvenile Correctional Facility for breaking and entering. Doctors had diagnosed him with several mental health illnesses, including bipolar disorder (a condition in which people alternate between deep depression and mania). During his time

Keeping Mentally Ill Youth out of Prison

For thirteen years Donetta Foxx watched as her adopted son was repeatedly transferred from school to hospital to prison because of an undiagnosed mental illness. Her son saw doctor after doctor, but none was able to help.

Then, in 2009, a juvenile justice worker recommended a Dane County, Wisconsin, program called Children Come First, which helps mentally ill children stay at home while getting the mental health treatment they need. The organization's coordinators develop a personalized treatment program for each child. They also work with schools and the court system to ensure all of the child's needs are met—a management process that is known as wraparound care. Children Come First says it was able to reduce the number of kids going into jail from an average of seventy per day in 2006 to less than thirty per day in 2014. Programs like Children Come First also saved the state of Wisconsin an estimated $6.5 million that it would have otherwise spent on residential mental health programs. Without this program, "I'm sure certainly he'd be in jail, if not dead or something else," Foxx says of her son. "But we had enough netting around him to keep him stable to adulthood."

Quoted in Adam Rodewald, Alison Dirr, and Rory Linnane, "Justice Advocates Cite State as Treatment Model," *Post-Crescent*, March 17, 2016. www.postcrescent.com.

at the facility, Donald assaulted a guard, repeatedly got into fights with other inmates, cut his arms with pencils, and dismembered a bird he had caught. Though the prison gave him mood-stabilizing drugs, it lacked the resources to get him the counseling and other mental health services he needed.

Mental health programs in youth prisons are scarce because money to pay for them is equally scarce. The programs that do exist do not always do a good job of addressing young people's emotional needs. Kids with mental health issues who do not get treatment in prison are more likely to commit crimes and end up back in jail after they are released.

Budget constraints prevent young inmates with mental health and substance abuse issues from getting the treatment they need to recover and stay out of prison. Youth facilities also lag far behind the public school system in giving kids the academic and vocational skills they need to make it on the outside and avoid re-incarceration. Though some prisons provide job training and arts programs, they are often limited because of funding. Yet a few programs are trying to help reintegrate young people into their communities after prison, and at least some of them have been very successful.

Chapter 5

Finding a New Path Forward

Young people who serve their time and follow the rules can eventually hope to walk free again. But what awaits them once they cross back through the barbed-wire prison fence? Each year about one hundred thousand young people leave the juvenile justice system. In many cases, they have spent nearly one-third of their lives in a prison-like setting. For those who are newly released, the reality of life on the outside is not always rosy.

Often kids are discharged back into the same turbulent, dangerous situations that brought them to prison in the first place. They return home to families struggling with poverty, substance abuse, domestic violence, and untreated mental health issues. They come back to crime-filled neighborhoods. Those who are under eighteen may be sent back to failing high schools that cannot adequately prepare them for college and a future career.

The outlook can be even worse for kids who do not have a family to take them back in after prison. In California, 70 percent of all state prison inmates have spent time in the foster care system. At age eighteen, foster kids age out of the system, meaning they are too old to live with another family. After prison, they are on their own. More than a third of foster youth who are released from California prisons become homeless within eighteen months of their release.

Even when young people do have a family to return to after prison, they may not have a place to live. When young people who live in public housing are arrested, their crime can get their whole family evicted, even before they are convicted of a crime. This so-called one-strike housing policy can drive families apart. "Parents are asked to banish their teenage children from their

When young people exit the barbed-wire enclosures and leave behind the rigidly structured existence of a detention center or prison, they often do not know what awaits them. Having a supportive family improves chances for success.

own home," says Jamie Kalven, founder of the Invisible Institute, a Chicago-based organization that aims to hold public institutions accountable for human rights offenses. "A kid caught with a joint in his pocket will trigger this draconian process."[61]

Landlords of private apartments and homes are sometimes unwilling to rent to someone who has a prison past. People with criminal records are not protected under the Fair Housing Act, which prevents landlords from turning people down on the basis of their religion, gender, ethnic background, or disability.

No Services

Formerly incarcerated youth may be denied other services too. Johnny Waller Jr. was eighteen years old in 1998, when he was convicted on felony drug charges. In 2001 he was released from prison. Waller tried to get back on his feet, but he could not get a federal loan to help him pay for college, and he was rejected every time he applied for work. He started his own janitorial company, and he did well for a while. Then, in 2007, Waller had to take time off from work when his young son, Jordyn, was diagnosed with stomach cancer. As the bills for Jordyn's treatment mounted, Waller applied for food stamps, but he was denied because of something he did "when I was 18 years old that didn't have anything to do with my son." He lamented, "I really needed assistance there."[62]

In 1996 the federal government passed a welfare reform law that prevented felons with drug convictions (but not convictions for other offenses) from getting welfare or food stamps. Some states have since eased or overturned these restrictions, but others have not. Young people who have been arrested for certain offenses, including drugs or alcohol, may even have their driver's license suspended. Without a means of transportation, they can find it hard to get to a job or attend school.

A few programs are trying to provide more educational opportunities for people once they leave prison. In July 2015 the Department of Education and the Justice Department introduced the Second Chance Pell Pilot Program. This program offers formerly incarcerated Americans Pell Grants—money that they can use toward a college education without having to repay.

No Jobs

Serving time is in many ways like a brand. Employers are reluctant to hire someone who has a criminal record. After Johnny Waller's release from prison, he applied for 175 jobs and did not get a single one of them. In addition to facing discrimination because of their past crimes, young people who have spent most of their lives in prison may lack the education and skills needed to perform all but the most basic jobs.

In 2013 Gary Durant was released from a California prison after serving nearly seven years for a gang-related killing he had taken part in at age seventeen. As he left the prison, he was handed seventy dollars and a bus ticket back to his home, Washington,

DC. Then he was on his own. "I got locked up for murder at 17 for hanging with the wrong group of people," he says. "Hanging with the wrong group of people can mess your whole life up." Once he arrived home, Durant looked for work, but it was not easy to find. He got lucky when a doggy day care center owner was willing to overlook his criminal record and offered him a job earning nine dollars an hour. Durant used the opportunity to try to turn his life around. "I used to be a boy but now I'm a man. A man with goals and a man that plans to live and not to ever become that used to be person again."[63]

In a 2015 survey by the Ella Baker Center for Human Rights, 76 percent of former inmates said they found it difficult or almost impossible to find a job. Nearly two-thirds were unemployed or underemployed (meaning they did not have enough paid work to support themselves) five years after their release. "Once you're in that system, it's like quicksand—you can't get out,"[64] says Tara Libert, co-founder of Free Minds, an organization that helps young inmates reenter society after their release.

> "I used to be a boy but now I'm a man. A man with goals and a man that plans to live and not to ever become that used to be person again."[63]
>
> —Former youth inmate Gary Durant.

Without access to school, a job, or the services they need to survive, many formerly incarcerated young people struggle to get by. "It was very hard for me coming home," says Jabriera Handy, who was jailed on charges of murder and assault in her grandmother's death. "It seemed like everything was spiraling down. I wasn't able to get a job. I wasn't able to attend school. I wasn't able to even get things from the department of juvenile services. I didn't have a place to stay."[65]

Those who cannot find paying work often resort to criminal enterprises. "When a man doesn't have a job, he needs to make money somehow. . . . It might be legally or illegally,"[66] comments Mark Sinski, program coordinator at Genesis, a Milwaukee, Wisconsin, organi-

Youths at an Illinois juvenile detention center take part in small engine classes. Vocational programs for inmates—and also for former inmates—can help them find jobs once they return to their communities.

zation that helps people readjust to life after prison. About 40 percent of people who are released from prisons in the United States each year end up back in jail for another crime within three years, according to a 2013 study by the Rand Corporation.

States and private organizations have stepped in to help former inmates find work. Louisiana's Re-Entry Court program teaches young inmates trades such as plumbing, welding, and the culinary arts. Pioneer Human Services in Seattle, Washington, offers job training, interview skills, apprenticeships, and job-finding assistance to former inmates. "Our case managers work around the clock to help people with all of their needs," says Nanette Sorich, a Pioneer spokesperson. "After they get hired . . . we have a case manager and job developer who works with them on their career path the first 12 months after they are hired to ensure their success."[67]

Sent Back to a Home They Never Knew

One group of young people who commit crimes and serve time sometimes finds that they will not be given a second chance. Under US law, youths who are in the country legally but are not citizens can be deported to the country of their birth. This is what happened to Jose (not his real name). At age sixteen he was sentenced to prison for attempted robbery. While in prison, he graduated from college and planned for his future career. Yet upon his release at age twenty-eight, he was immediately deported to Mexico—a country he had not visited since he was four years old.

Touch Hak also faced the threat of deportation after serving time for selling drugs. His family had fled Cambodia in the 1970s. They ended up in Stockton, California, where Hak became caught up in gangs and violence at a young age. At age thirty-eight, after his release from prison, he had found a factory job and was trying to turn his life around. But because of his criminal past, Hak was at risk of being deported to Cambodia. "How will I survive there?" he asked. "I'm a city boy. America is my home. I've lived here for 30 years."

Some civil libertarians argue that even noncitizens who have been incarcerated deserve the right to fight their deportation. "They have served their time and have been found to pose no public danger," says Joanne Lin, a legislative counsel for the American Civil Liberties Union. "We owe them a close review and due process, not a double punishment."

Quoted in Teresa Wiltz, "Southeast Asian Refugees and the Prison-Deportation Pipeline," PEW Charitable Trusts, April 5, 2016. www.pewtrusts.org.

Quoted in Pamela Constable, "For Non-U.S. Citizens, Early Release from Prison Means Swift Deportation," *Washington Post*, November 5, 2015. www.washingtonpost.com.

Feeling Anxious and Unsettled

When they are finally released from prison, many former inmates feel a mixture of joy and anxiety. While they look forward to their freedom, they also worry about rejoining a world that has gone on for many months or years without them. It can be disorienting to suddenly step out from the rigid, controlled prison system and into the unstructured world outside.

In prison, teens were given food and clothes. They were told when to wake up, eat, shower, go to school, and sleep. Once they are released, they have to start making their own decisions. Those who have been in prison for many years may have to learn even the most basic skills, such as how to use a smartphone or a subway card. They may lack the foundations they need to restart their lives—a bank account, an address, credit with which to get a loan, and a driver's license.

Those who are over eighteen and do not have family to pick them up might leave prison with nothing more than a suitcase and a few dollars to get them home. Then, suddenly, they are responsible for themselves—sometimes for the first time in their lives. "It's like being dropped on a deserted island and there's a hurricane coming," relates Bruce Hodge, a former inmate who served eighteen years in a Georgia prison for a murder committed when he was a teenager. "There's no support."[68]

Some former inmates return home to find that the people who once loved them have left them behind. "I have no family at all out here and I am completely on my own with $75 and nowhere to go," one man said of his release. "I was engaged when I got locked up at 18—now I'm 45, the rest of my teens, all of my 20s, 30s and most of my 40s gone!"[69]

Former inmates also have to live with the worry that any error in judgment or behavior could land them right back in prison. Some young people are so overwhelmed and scared of being back on the outside that they withdraw completely, refusing to rejoin society. For kids who worry about their future, reentry programs can mean the difference between transitioning back to a normal life and ending up in prison again.

Prison-to-Life Programs

To have the greatest chance of succeeding, youth need programs to help them transition from prison to home, school, and/or work. "In reentry, you really need a wraparound approach," explains Michelle Newell, a senior policy associate at the Children's Defense

Fund, an organization that helps raise children out of poverty and protect them from neglect and abuse. "It's really about building up their self-confidence and providing hope and a sense of what their path can be."[70]

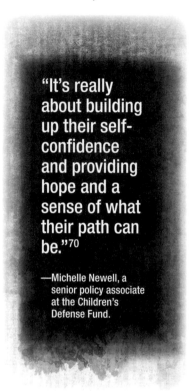

After prison, young people need a safe, stable place to live. They need a plan to help them transition back to school or into vocational training. Some need substance abuse counseling or mental health care. Others need to learn basic life skills, such as goal setting and problem solving. And all of them need positive adult guidance and supervision to prevent them from getting in trouble again. Often that supervision comes in the form of a caseworker, who serves as a liaison between the youth and the prison, family, and school. "The stronger relationships with a teacher or a counselor or a community-based organizer, the more successful they will be back home,"[71] Newell says.

Research finds that effective reentry programs can help prevent young people from ending up back in prison. In Chicago, a child and family services organization called Children's Home and Aid offers a program to reintegrate youth after they are released from prison, with the goal of keeping them out of the justice system in the future. As teens leave area juvenile detention facilities, they get a case manager and a therapist, who help them set goals and find the services they need to manage the issues that originally led to their incarceration. "It might be drug treatment or anger management, individual counseling or family counseling, we even have the ability to get creative and do art therapy,"[72] says Mark Smith, a delinquency supervisor at Children's Home and Aid. A similar program, called Redeploy Illinois, provides mental health care, life skills, and other types of treatment to young people in the state's criminal justice system. Since 2005 the organization has helped 1,309 youths avoid incarceration.

Offering Alternatives to Prison

While some nonprofit organizations work to help kids transition out of prison, other organizations are trying to reform the juvenile justice system entirely. Their goal is to prevent young people from ending up in jail in the first place.

Some of these organizations offer programs that provide services long before kids commit crimes. For example, they may address poverty in the community or increase educational opportunities for at-risk kids. The Children's Defense Fund offers a number of youth development programs aimed at preventing violence and getting kids excited about learning so they do not drop out of school and get into trouble. Many of these programs are aimed at minorities to stop the cycle of African American and Hispanic youths being jailed in disproportionately high numbers compared to white youths.

Other organizations, such as the Juvenile Detention Alternatives Initiative, want to institute more rigorous screening when

A Lucas County (Ohio) Juvenile Court judge presides over a meeting with a juvenile offender in 2015. The county has instituted a screening program to keep nonviolent youth out of prison.

How the Government Is Helping Youth in Prison

There was a time when the criminal justice system punished kids as if they were miniature adults. Gradually the system started to recognize that young people have special developmental needs that may not be met in jail.

One recent movement has been to end the use of solitary confinement for the youngest inmates. In 2016 President Barack Obama announced that he would ban the use of solitary for young people in federal prisons. In a January 25, 2016, editorial that appeared in the *Washington Post*, Obama discussed Kalief Browder, a young man who spent nearly two years in solitary confinement at Rikers Island and later committed suicide. "How can we subject prisoners to unnecessary solitary confinement, knowing its effects, and then expect them to return to our communities as whole people? It doesn't make us safer. It's an affront to our common humanity." The president also announced plans to help young people expunge, or clear, their criminal records so they can get access to public housing, education, and employment.

Barack Obama, "Why We Must Rethink Solitary Confinement," *Washington Post*, January 25, 2016. www .washingtonpost.com.

kids are first arrested. Their goal is to separate young people who are violent and pose a real threat to their communities from those who are nonviolent and do not pose a risk to public safety. The latter group can then be steered toward community services and avoid prison time. This kind of screening program has worked in Ohio. In 1998 the Lucas County Juvenile Court in Toledo sent more than three hundred young people to state prisons. Then the town introduced an assessment center to screen young offenders and place those who do not pose a real risk into the community instead of putting them in prison. As a result of the screening program, in 2014 the county's juvenile court sent only seventeen young people to prison.

Another movement within the juvenile justice system supports alternatives to prison for young people who do get into trouble. The National Juvenile Justice Network helps ensure that youths have access to lawyers who are experienced in representing young people and can effectively fight for their rights. They also work to keep young offenders in their homes and communities rather than sending them off to lockup facilities far away. Young people are offered services such as mentoring, counseling, family therapy, and mental health and substance abuse treatment to keep them out of trouble. Treating young people at home is less expensive than putting them in prisons, and research finds that it can be a more effective way to prevent them from committing future crimes.

Several states, including Kentucky, Ohio, Texas, Missouri, and Hawaii, have reformed their juvenile justice systems and have reduced the use of prison time for young people. Ohio has replaced its large prison-style juvenile correctional facilities with smaller community-based ones. In 2012 New York started an initiative called Close to Home to keep delinquent youths near their families while they get the supervision and services they need to stay out of trouble.

An End to Youth Prisons?

Some organizations are trying to go even further. They want to see every juvenile prison and detention facility in the country shut down forever. These groups believe prison is not the right place for young people. They argue that keeping youths out of prison is not only more effective but also can save states a lot of money. Locking up a juvenile can cost nearly $150,000 a year. The indirect expenses of youth incarceration, which include future lost wages and public assistance, cost taxpayers between $8 billion and $21 billion annually, according to data from the Justice Policy Institute. "I believe it's long past time to close these inhumane, ineffective, wasteful factories of failure once and for all. Every one of them," asserts Patrick McCarthy, president of the Annie E. Casey Foundation, which promotes juvenile justice reform. "We need to admit that what we're doing doesn't work, and is making the problem worse while costing billions of dollars and ruining thousands of lives."[73]

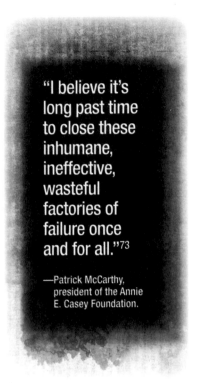

"I believe it's long past time to close these inhumane, ineffective, wasteful factories of failure once and for all."[73]

—Patrick McCarthy, president of the Annie E. Casey Foundation.

Thanks to new programs and government policies, the number of incarcerated youths has dropped sharply over the last couple of decades. Between 1997 and 2011, the overall rate of prison sentencing for young people fell by around 50 percent, according to a 2015 report by the Council of State Governments Justice Center. Some states, like Connecticut and Rhode Island, saw a nearly 80 percent drop in imprisonment rates. The number of juveniles locked up in the United States plunged from more than 108,000 in 2000 to 66,000 in 2010.

Most experts agree that prison is not the right place for the majority of young inmates. Prisons are expensive and filled with violence and abuse, and they often do not provide the kind of education, mental health care, and other services young people need to get out of the criminal justice system and succeed in life. Over the last couple of decades there has been a movement from both governments and nonprofit organizations to reform existing youth prisons to make life better for those who are incarcerated and to provide services young people need to transition from prison to society. The even stronger push in the future may be to get rid of these facilities entirely and to move the focus from incarcerating young people to rehabilitating them.

Source Notes

Introduction: Locked Up and Alone

1. Quoted in Benjamin Weiser and Michael Schwirtz, "U.S. Inquiry Finds a 'Culture of Violence' Against Teenage Inmates at Rikers Island," *New York Times*, August 4, 2014. www.nytimes.com.
2. Quoted in Trey Bundy, "Sixteen, Alone, 23 Hours a Day, in a Six-by-Eight-Foot Box," Medium, March 5, 2014. https://medium.com.
3. Quoted in Bundy, "Sixteen, Alone, 23 Hours a Day, in a Six-by-Eight-Foot Box."
4. Ismael Nazario, "What I Learned as a Kid in Jail," TED, November 2014. www.ted.com.
5. Nazario, "What I Learned as a Kid in Jail."

Chapter 1: The Path from School to Prison

6. Quoted in Nicholas St. John Green, *Criminal Law Reports: Being Reports of Cases Determined in the Federal and State Courts of the United States, and in the Courts of England, Ireland, Canada, Etc. with Notes.* Vol. 1. New York: Hurd and Houghton, 1876, p. 400.
7. Equal Justice Initiative, "The Superpredator Myth, 20 Years Later," April 7, 2014. www.eji.org.
8. *New York Times*, "The 'Superpredator' Scare," April 6, 2014. www.nytimes.com.
9. Quoted in Eliza Shapiro, "In 'Juvenile in Justice,' Children Caught in America's Prison System," Daily Beast, October 21, 2012. www.thedailybeast.com.
10. Quoted in Erik Eckholm, "A Murderer at 14, Then a Lifer, Now a Man Pondering a Future," *New York Times*, April 10, 2015. www.nytimes.com.
11. Quoted in LA Youth, "Behind Bars: Four Teens in Prison Tell Their Stories," March/April 2000. www.layouth.com.

12. Quoted in LA Youth, "Behind Bars."
13. Quoted in Jackie Mader, "Pipeline to Prison: Special Education Too Often Leads to Jail for Thousands of American Children," *Washington Monthly*, October 26, 2014. www.washingtonmonthly.com.
14. Quoted in Calamari Productions, "Young Kids, Hard Time: Director's Cut," YouTube, June 5, 2012. www.youtube.com /watch?v=g3lw6PMjj40.
15. Quoted in Campaign for Youth Justice, "YJAM Recap 2015: Sharing Stories, Why We Start with Stories, and Move Them to Action," October 29, 2015. www.campaignforyouthjustice .org.

Chapter 2: Freedom Lost

16. *Teen in Jail* (blog), "A Prisoner's First Day," September 24, 2009. http://teeninjail.blogspot.com.
17. Quoted in CFYJ Juvenile Justice, "Collateral Consequences: The Story of Jabriera Handy, Juvenile Justice Advocate," YouTube, October 20, 2015. www.youtube.com/watch?v=Tazx QU5H2HU.
18. Quoted in Calamari Productions, "Young Kids, Hard Time: Director's Cut," YouTube, June 5, 2012. www.youtube.com/ watch?v=g3lw6PMjj40.
19. Judicial Branch of Arizona, County of Mohave, "Probation Department—Serving Time in a Juvenile Detention Facility." www.mohavecourts.com.
20. Quoted in *Teen in Jail* (blog), "No Privacy," January 13, 2010. http://teeninjail.blogspot.com.
21. Quoted in Anna Merlan, "While Awaiting Trial, Teens in Dallas County Jail Being Kept in Their Cells 23 Hours a Day," *Dallas Observer*, July 30, 2012. www.dallasobserver.com.
22. Quoted in *Frontline,* "Profile: Andrew Medina," PBS. www .pbs.org.
23. Quoted in Aviva Stahl, "In a Maryland Jail, Teens Charged as Adults Face Isolation and Neglect," Solitary Watch, June 17, 2014. http://solitarywatch.com.

24. Quoted in American Civil Liberties Union, "Growing Up Locked Down: Youth in Solitary Confinement in Jails and Prisons Across the United States," October 2012. www.aclu.org.
25. Quoted in Dana Liebelson, "This Is What Happens When We Lock Children in Solitary Confinement," *Mother Jones*, January/February 2015. www.motherjones.com.
26. American Civil Liberties Union, "Growing Up Locked Down."
27. Quoted in LA Youth, "Behind Bars."
28. Stephen Katz, "What It's Like to Actually Eat the Food in Oakland County Jail," *Detroit MetroTimes*, July 8, 2015. www.metrotimes.com.
29. Katz, "What It's Like to Actually Eat the Food in Oakland County Jail."
30. Quoted in Orange County Government, "Teen Talk." http://ocgov.com.
31. Quoted in LA Youth, "Behind Bars."
32. Quoted in LA Youth, "Behind Bars."
33. Quoted in Scott Smith, "For Youth Inmates, Family Visits Key in Rehabilitation," Recordnet.com, April 7, 2007. www.recordnet.com.
34. Quoted in Smith, "For Youth Inmates, Family Visits Key in Rehabilitation."

Chapter 3: Finding Allies

35. Quoted in Human Rights Watch, "Life Without Parole in Adult Prison." www.hrw.org.
36. Quoted in Anne Nurse, *Locked Up, Locked Out: Young Men in the Juvenile Justice System*. Nashville: Vanderbilt University Press, 2010, p. 105.
37. Quoted in Campaign for Youth Justice, "YJAM Recap 2015."
38. Quoted in Lora Lempert, *Women Doing Life: Gender, Punishment, and the Struggle for Identity.* New York: New York University Press, 2016, p. 201.
39. Quoted in Christi Stevens, "Gangs a Constant Worry in Juvenile Detention Facility," CYC-Net. www.cyc-net.org.

40. Quoted in John Caniglia, "More than 40 Heartless Felons, a Fast Growing and Violent Gang, Expected to Face Major Charges in Cuyahoga County," Cleveland.com, June 12, 2014. www.cleveland.com.

41. Quoted in Jason Carroll, "Growing Up Behind Bars: Life in Prison for Teens," *American Morning* (blog), CNN, March 16, 2010. http://am.blogs.cnn.com.

42. Quoted in Julie K. Brown, "*Miami Herald* Investigation: Yount Inmates Beaten and Raped in Prison Broomstick Ritual," *Miami Herald*, September 12, 2015. www.miamiherald.com.

43. John Lash, "The Hidden Culture of Prison Violence," Juvenile Justice Information Exchange, May 11, 2012. http://jjie.org.

44. Quoted in Joel Rose, "'Culture of Violence' Pervades Rikers' Juvenile Facilities," NPR, October 15, 2014. www.npr.org.

45. Quoted in Brad Hamilton, "Brutal System of Teen Beatings Continues at Rikers Island's RNDC Prison," *New York Post*, May 6, 2012. http://nypost.com.

46. Quoted in Rose, "'Culture of Violence' Pervades Rikers' Juvenile Facilities."

47. Quoted in Michigan Live, "Video Depositions: 7 Inmates Share Their Stories of Sexual Abuse Behind Bars," April 14, 2015. www.mlive.com.

48. Quoted in Joaquin Sapien, "Rape and Other Sexual Violence Prevalent in Juvenile Justice System," ProPublica, June 6, 2013. www.propublica.org.

49. John Lash, "Beyond the Horrible, the Reality of Sexual Assault in Youth Detention," Juvenile Justice Information Exchange, April 20, 2012. http://jjie.org.

50. Quoted in Zusha Elinson, "Juveniles Sexually Abused by Staffers at Correctional Facilities," *Wall Street Journal*, January 1, 2015. www.wsj.com.

Chapter 4: Preparing for Life on the Outside

51. Quoted in Sarah Butrymowicz, "Pipeline to Prison: How the Juvenile Justice System Fails Special Education Students," *Washington Monthly*, October 26, 2014. www.washingtonmonthly.com.

52. Quoted in Alyssa Morones, "Juvenile-Justice System Not Meeting Educational Needs, Report Says," *Education Week*, April 17, 2014. www.edweek.org.
53. Quoted in Butrymowicz, "Pipeline to Prison."
54. Quoted in Erica L. Green, "Criticism Leveled at Schools for Maryland Juvenile Offenders," *Baltimore Sun*, December 28, 2015. www.baltimoresun.com.
55. Quoted in Butrymowicz, "Pipeline to Prison."
56. Shannon, "It Happened to Me: I Teach in a Juvenile Correctional Center," XO Jane, October 17, 2012. www.xojane.com.
57. Quoted in Chris Megerian, "N.J. Prisons Teaching Inmates Job Skills to Avoid Return to Life of Crime," NJ.com, December 29, 2009. www.nj.com.
58. Quoted in Melissa Wynne-Jones, "A Step to Ending the Youth-to-Prison Pipeline—New Earth's Programs Reduce the LA County Youth Recidivism Rate from 80% to 5%," Popular Resistance, July 24, 2014. www.popularresistance.org.
59. Quoted in Human Rights Watch, "Life Without Parole in Adult Prison."
60. Quoted in Solomon Moore, "Mentally Ill Offenders Strain Juvenile System," *New York Times*, August 9, 2009. www.nytimes.com.

Chapter 5: Finding a New Path Forward

61. Quoted in Susie Allen, "Conference Examines Consequences of Criminal Activity Eviction from Public Housing," UChicago News, June 11, 2015. http://news.uchicago.edu.
62. Quoted in Rebecca Beitsch, "Rethinking Restrictions on Food Stamps and Welfare Benefits for Drug Felons," Flagler Live, August 3, 2015. http://flaglerlive.com.
63. Quoted in Theresa Vargas, "In D.C., Life After Prison Poses Extra Challenges for Youths Cnvicted as Adults," *Washington Post*, September 28, 2013. www.washingtonpost.com.
64. Quoted in Vargas, "In D.C., Life After Prison Poses Extra Challenges for Youths Convicted as Adults."

65. Quoted in CFYJ Juvenile Justice, "Collateral Consequences."

66. Quoted in Rick Barrett, "Out of Prison, Out of Work: Ex-Inmates Face Struggles After Release," *Journal Sentinel*, March 29, 2015. www.jsonline.com.

67. Quoted in Matt Ferner, "These Programs Are Helping Prisoners Live Again on the Outside," Huffington Post, September 9, 2015. www.huffingtonpost.com.

68. Quoted in Ryan Schill and Clay Duda, "Boys Growing Up to Be Boys: Mandatory Minimums and Teens in Adult Prisons," Juvenile Justice Information Exchange, March 25, 2013. http://jjie.org.

69. Quoted in Marpessa Kupuendua, "Coming Home: Revelations from Former Prisoners," *BayView*, April 12, 2011. http://sfbayview.com.

70. Quoted in Elly Yu, "Life After Juvenile Detention," Juvenile Justice Information Exchange, May 23, 2014. http://jjie.org.

71. Quoted in Yu, "Life After Juvenile Detention."

72. Quoted in Sarah Baraba, "Community Programs Keep Youth Out of Prison and Help Them Return to Community," Juvenile Justice Initiative, August 17, 2012. http://jjustice.org.

73. Quoted in Shaena Fazal, "A Much-Needed Alternative to Youth Prisons," Huffington Post, July 15, 2015. www.huffingtonpost.com.

Organizations to Contact

Annie E. Casey Foundation
701 St. Paul St.
Baltimore, MD 21202
phone: (410) 547-6600
website: www.aecf.org

The Annie E. Casey Foundation works to strengthen families and communities so that the young people who live within them have a greater chance for success.

Campaign for the Fair Sentencing of Youth
phone: (202) 289-4677
website: http://fairsentencingofyouth.org

This organization is trying to end life sentences for youth under age eighteen and to provide more effective alternatives to prison sentences.

Center for Children's Law and Policy
1701 K St. NW, Suite 1100
Washington, DC 20006
phone: (202) 637-0377
website: http://cclp.org

The Center for Children's Law and Policy does research and advocates for the rights of children in the criminal justice system.

Children's Defense Fund
25 E St. NW
Washington, DC 20001
phone: (800) 233-1200
website: www.childrensdefense.org

This organization advocates for the needs of America's children. It promotes preventive programs to help kids stay in school and keep out of trouble.

Justice Policy Institute

1012 14th St. NW, Suite 600
Washington, DC 20005
phone: (202) 558-7974
website: http://justicepolicy.org

This group tries to change policies to reduce incarceration and promote the well-being of at-risk individuals.

National Juvenile Justice Network (NJJN)

1319 F St. NW, Suite 402
Washington, DC 20004
phone: (202) 467-0864
website: www.njjn.org

The NJJN works to change state and federal laws and policies to reform the juvenile justice system for the benefit of America's youth.

For Further Research

Books
Nancy A. Heitzeg, *The School-to-Prison Pipeline: Education, Discipline, and Racialized Double Standards*. Santa Barbara, CA: ABC-CLIO, 2016.

Susan Madden, *Born, Not Raised: Voices from Juvenile Hall*. San Diego: Human Exposures, 2013.

Ashley Nellis, *A Return to Justice: Rethinking Our Approach to Juveniles in the System*. Lanham, MD: Rowman & Littlefield, 2016.

Jean Trounstine, *Boy with a Knife: A Story of Murder, Remorse, and a Prisoner's Fight for Justice*. New York: Ig, 2016.

Paul Volponi, *Rikers High*. New York: Viking, 2010.

Internet Sources
American Civil Liberties Union, "Fact Sheet on the Juvenile Justice System." www.aclu.org/aclu-fact-sheet-juvenile-justice-system.

Campaign for Youth Justice, "Jails, Prisons, and Juveniles." www.campaignforyouthjustice.org/images/presskit/factsheet.pdf.

Jessica Lahey, "The Steep Costs of Keeping Juveniles in Adult Prisons," *Atlantic*, January 8, 2016. www.theatlantic.com/education/archive/2016/01/the-cost-of-keeping-juveniles-in-adult-prisons/423201.

National Association for the Advancement of Colored People, "Criminal Justice Fact Sheet." www.naacp.org/pages/criminal-justice-fact-sheet.

Websites
American Civil Liberties Union (www.aclu.org). This group works to preserve every American's rights and liberties under the US Constitution and the nation's laws.

Corporation for National and Community Service (www.nationalservice.gov). This federal agency helps millions of Americans improve their lives through service projects. It includes Youth Opportunity AmeriCorps, which specifically helps formerly incarcerated young people find work.

Council of State Governments Justice Center (http://csgjusticecenter.org). The Justice Center is a nonprofit organization that helps governments implement strategies to both safeguard the public and strengthen communities.

Pew Charitable Trusts (www.pewtrusts.org). This organization releases reports—including documents on youth incarceration—that help inform the public and improve government policies.

Volunteers of America (www.voa.org). This organization helps people rebuild their lives after prison, homelessness, addiction, and other setbacks. It helps more than 2 million people in forty-six states.

Index

Picture Credits

Cover: Thinkstock Images

6: Associated Press

10: Maury Aaseng

13: Depositphotos

17: Associated Press

22: Dean hanson/Journal/ ZUMApress/Newscom

26: Associated Press

31: 2004 Tyrone Turner-Black Star/Newscom

35: Associated Press

38: Associated Press

41: Associated Press

45: Skip O'Rourke/ZUMApress/Newscom

49: Associated Press

50: Associated Press

56: Associated Press

59: Antonio Perez/MCT/Newscom

63: Associated Press